SOUTH AFRICA

1

The massive sandstone bulk of Table Mountain (1), flanked by Devil's Peak, Lion's Head and Signal Hill, provides a magnificent backdrop to the oldest, and arguably the most attractive, of South African cities. Cape Town owes its very existence to Table Mountain, as it was the freshwater streams running off the mountain slopes which prompted early explorers to anchor in tempestuous Table Bay and set up a halfway station for ships sailing between Europe and the East. Today the spectacular mountain, which ranks among the world's best known landmarks, draws more than half a million people to its summit each year and is one of the most climbed peaks in the world. Most visitors, however, prefer to take the awe-inspiring, two-minute trip in the cable way (3) up to the station

2

3

4

5

at the top of the mountain, from where the view of the city and its surroundings is truly sensational. On the edge of the city bowl, below Table Mountain, lies the vibrant and exciting Victoria and Alfred Waterfront (2). Another of the city's premier tourist attractions, the Waterfront boasts an oceanarium, several museums, shops, cinemas, restaurants, bars, open quaysides and bustling public squares. Boat trips take tourists to Robben Island and cruise along the peninsula's magnificent shoreline.

The white, sandy beaches of the Cape Peninsula and the mountains tumbling down to the ocean are a major draw for visitors to the city. Clifton (4), with its granite outcrops and wide beach, is situated on the Atlantic seaboard and is one of the more popular beaches.

Cape Town is also a paradise of modern shopping malls, emporiums, bazaars, stores and open-air markets such as the cobblestoned and leafy Green Market Square (5). At the start of each new year, the city streets come alive to the sound of singing accompanied by banjos, drums, whistles and a brass band, as the coloured community, dressed in vivid costumes, parade through the town celebrating their culture with the Coon Carnival (6).

6

7

Looking out towards the hinterland, from the slopes of Devil's Peak, is the memorial to Cecil John Rhodes (7). A ruthless visionary and financial genius, Rhodes came out from Britain to South Africa as a young man, whereupon he rose to fame by taking control of the country's international diamond trade. Later he established himself as a politician and empire-builder, and from 1890 to 1896 he served as Prime Minister of the Cape.

Situated further along the east-facing slopes of the Table Mountain chain, overlooking the Cape Flats, is the Kirstenbosch National Botanical Garden (8). The variety of plants found in the Western Cape is almost unrivalled, and these gardens are a wonderland of glorious indigenous flower displays, trees and shrubs.

8

9

10

11

12

Cape Point is located at the southernmost extremity of the Cape Peninsula (9 and 10) and is commonly, but inaccurately, held to be the meeting place of the Atlantic and Indian oceans. Cape Point is part of the Cape of Good Hope Nature Reserve, a 7 750-hectare sanctuary protecting the region's unique flora – the fynbos. It is off this headland that many sightings have been recorded of the Flying Dutchman, a ghost ship destined to sail the seas until Judgement Day. During good weather visitors can wander along the numerous paths and explore the reserve.

Hugging the shoreline of False Bay are a collection of small towns and fishing villages. The small harbour at Kalk (lime) Bay (11) still shelters the town's weathered fishing fleet from the batterings of the Cape storms. This bay takes its name from the days when sea-shells were once baked near the shore in large kilns to produce lime.

The winding ten-kilometre road along Chapman's Peak Drive (12) is one of the most dramatic in the country as the mountains drop straight into the sea. The road clings to the mountainside with only a narrow retaining wall protecting motorists from a sheer fall into the deep waters far below.

The Cape Peninsula is home to hundreds of chacma baboons (13), which can often be seen grooming each other alongside the roads while watching the cars go by. They frequent the car parks in and around the Cape of Good Hope Nature Reserve where they have become a nuisance because people persist in feeding them. Hikers and ramblers walking in the mountains can sometimes hear the baboons barking from high up in the rocky outcrops or see groups of them foraging among the fynbos in search of food and water.

13

14

15

16

The Cape has long been associated with fine wines. In 1685, one of the first Dutch governors to the Cape, Simon van der Stel, founded what was to become the famous wine estate called Constantia (14). After his death in 1712, the land was divided up but the heart of the estate was retained at Groot (big) Constantia – van der Stel's magnificent homestead. This beautiful house is the oldest in the Cape and is built with thick white-washed walls, a thatched roof and ornate gables. It is a superb example of traditional Cape Dutch style architecture and has been preserved as a national monument. The house, with its exquisite period furniture, is a museum, as is the old wine cellar with its displays of antique wine drinking and storage vessels. Both Groot Constantia and the nearby Klein (small) Constantia – a remnant of van der Stel's original estate – are well known for their superior quality wines.

A short distance from Cape Town is the area known as the Cape Winelands. This region encompasses many wineries and estates of stunning beauty set amongst glorious mountains, cold river streams and steep valleys. The historic towns, such as Stellenbosch and Franschhoek, serve the surrounding winelands as well as the many visitors who pass through the lush vine-covered valleys to taste the famous local wines and enjoy the hospitality of the 200-year-old homesteads nestling beneath the mountains.

Franschhoek is the original home of the French Huguenots who fled to the Cape in order to escape Catholic persecution in France. Building on the experience they had gained in the vineyards of France, the Huguenots were instrumental in nurturing the wine culture in South Africa. The Huguenot Monument (15) was built in 1943 to commemorate the contribution the Huguenots made to South Africa. The

17

18

monument depicts a woman standing with a Bible in her right hand and a broken chain in her left, symbolising freedom from religious oppression. At the time when the Huguenots settled in the Franschhoek valley it was teeming with game, and herds of wild elephant used to migrate annually into the area via the Franschhoek mountain range.

Stellenbosch, in the heart of the winelands, is the second oldest town in South Africa (after Cape Town). Although it has grown to be the centre of a considerable wine and spirits industry, visitors can still walk along the leafy, oak-shaded streets and enjoy the unique charm of this relaxed town with its delightful examples of Cape Dutch, Georgian, Victorian and Regency style architectures. Oom Samie se Winkel (16), a Victorian-styled general store, is set in an historic avenue in which almost the entire street has become a national monument. The shop is one of Stellenbosch's most popular landmarks and sells spices, tobacco, dried fish and an assortment of products made in the traditional Afrikaans manner.

In the past, most of the country's winelands were situated in the fertile valleys near Cape Town, but today they extend to the fringes of the Karoo Desert. Approaching the winelands from the northern desert areas, you will pass through the dramatic Hex River Valley (17), one of the most spectacular gateways into the Cape Winelands. After the first cold spells of winter the snow-capped mountains provide an impressive backdrop to the vineyards and farmlands cradled in the valley below.

The Cape's southern coast offers some of the world's best land-based opportunities for watching whales. Hermanus, a popular holiday village on the shores of Walker Bay, sits atop a long line of cliffs, which makes it ideal for whale spotting. Hermanus was originally a whaling port and the Old Harbour (18) used to be a thriving centre of the fishing industry. The harbour has been preserved and houses a museum at the old stone fishing basin. On display are some of the harpoons that were used to kill the gentle giants of the sea.

These days the arrival of the whales is celebrated with a whale festival, usually held in mid-September when whale watching is at its finest. Towards the end of winter, with the onset of spring, the great marine mammals make their way in to shore to mate and give birth to their calves. Their arrival at the coast every year is heralded by Hermanus' whale crier (19), complete with sandwich board and kelp horn. A whale hotline provides visitors with information relating to the best places to spot whales.

The whales most likely to be seen are the Southern Right Whales (20). They can easily be viewed from a number of the villages along the coast, but particularly from Hermanus. These whales often come within 30 metres of the coastline, blowing plumes of water into the sky.

19

20

21

22

23

24

Extending for 230 kilometres along the southern seaboard is the Garden Route, one of the more entrancing coastlines, consisting of unspoilt beaches, secluded bays, lagoons, inland lakes, densely wooded mountain slopes, coves and estuaries. A charming old Class 24 narrow gauge train line, called the Outeniqua Choo-Tjoe, links a number of holiday villages dotted along this coastline. The train crosses the Kaaimans River mouth (21) close to Wilderness, a seaside village famed for its long beaches and seven inland lakes.

Further on down the train line is the beautiful town of Knysna, a popular holiday destination and wonderful base from which to explore the rest of the Garden Route. Knysna is situated on a 17-kilometre lagoon, the entrance to which is guarded by two towering buttresses of rock known as the Knysna Heads (23). The town is flanked by indigenous forests of ancient stinkwood and yellowwood, much of which has been replanted with exotic commercial plantations in recent times. However, some of the original fern forests still remain (22). It is unlikely that you will come across the almost extinct forest elephant of which only one of the

25

original herd is left. Visitors should look out for the brilliantly plumed, but extremely shy, Knysna lourie (25) that can be seen around the town.

Plettenberg Bay (24) is the area's foremost beach holiday destination, the white sand and warm, clear water drawing sun worshippers from afar. The bay is dominated by Beacon Island, a large holiday resort.

Inland from the Garden Route is the Little Karoo, a dry area which is home to the ostrich farming industry. Born out of the boom days in the 1890s when feathers were fashionable, the industry slumped at the outbreak of the First World War. It has since recovered and is flourishing today in and around the town of Oudtshoorn. At the turn of the century, prosperous feather merchants and buyers built elegant homes out of the local sandstone. Many of these feather palaces (26) still remain private homes, although some have been restored and are open to the public as museums. Enterprising ostrich farmers have also opened their doors to visitors and it is possible to tour the farms, learn about ostriches, watch jockeys race these large birds (29) and even ride one yourself.

Ostriches are not the only animals found in this area. The prehistoric crocodile (27) is another indigenous creature which is farmed commercially. A visit to the Cango Crocodile Ranch will give you an opportunity to see these enormous reptiles close up.

The Cango Caves (28), which are found at the foothills of the southern side of the Swartberg mountain range, consist of an extensive series of tunnels, chambers and strange dripstone formations. The outer caves of this natural limestone creation were probably first discovered by the San (Bushmen) who left their mark by decorating the walls with paintings of the wild animals they encountered there. Today it is a fairyland visited by many tourists.

26

27

28

29

30

31

The Swartberg mountain range divides the Little Karoo from the Great Karoo. Large, scorched flatlands broken only by dramatic mountain ranges and windblown koppies, such as those found in the famed Valley of Desolation (30), are characteristics of the Great Karoo. The valley, with its naturally eroded bizarre rock formations, is actually a cleft in the rock-strewn plateau and falls within the Karoo Nature Reserve.

Small, isolated hamlets are dotted throughout this dry region, serving the surrounding farming community. One of the best known and most historic of these is Graaff-Reinet, located 14 kilometres from the Valley of Desolation. This old frontier town has retained some of its former character from when the district was filled with hardy wanderers, hunters, explorers and pioneers. Many of the beautiful period buildings still stand, lending to the feeling of timelessness. Stretch Court (32), named

32

33

34

after Captain Charles Stretch who was the Government Surveyor of Graaff-Reinet in 1855, was perfectly restored in 1966.

Heading towards the coast and the Eastern Cape's largest urban city, Port Elizabeth, you will pass the Addo Elephant National Park. It was established in the early 1930s to preserve the remaining herds of Cape elephant. Having been hunted to near extinction, these elephants (31) have greatly recovered and flourish in the park alongside other wild animals and a fascinating diversity of flora.

The sea port city of Port Elizabeth was founded as a staging post for the British immigrants of 1820. It is now the thriving economic hub of the Eastern Cape and one of the major industrial centres of South Africa. This friendly city has maintained some of the old charming Victorian settler houses from days gone by, as seen in the beautifully restored terraced homes facing Donkin Street (33). There is much for the visitor to enjoy in Port Elizabeth. A world-class oceanarium renowned for its performing dolphins (34) and colourful variety of marine life is a favourite with visitors to the city.

Further north the coastline becomes more remote as you enter into Xhosa country and an area known as the Wild Coast – a landscape of rural Xhosa villages, rolling hills, spectacular land formations and thundering waterfalls. Here the Xhosa people go about their lives in their time-worn manner, the women smoking long pipes and wearing their splendid traditional head coverings (36).

One of the most distinctive natural features along this breathtaking coastline is the Hole-in-the-Wall (35), a massive detached cliff rising up from the sea in the form of an island at the mouth of the Mpako River. As the cliff is constantly battered by the crashing surf, a tunnel has formed in its centre through which the waves pound. The notoriously rough sea has made it the graveyard for a number of ships.

35

36

37

38

39

Durban's subtropical climate and sunny beaches, together with the warm waters of the Indian Ocean, make it a year-round holiday mecca (37). Protected by the Bluff, a low peninsula jutting out into the sea, the harbour mouth has seen thousands of ships pass in and out since the days when Durban was still known as Port Natal. Today Durban is South Africa's premier sea port and third largest metropolis.

Durban, more than any other city in South Africa, radiates the pulse and complex face of Africa. It is a vibrant city where visitors can mingle with a variety of locals, including white, Zulu and Indian people, in a colourful and cacophonous mix of hooting taxis, sidewalk merchants, buses and pedestrians. The Indian markets are abuzz with clamouring vendors trading fish, vegetables, souvenirs and other bric-à-brac, and exotic aromas emanate from the stalls of the spice sellers (39).

The hot weather is conducive to outdoor activities and dozens of open-air flea markets sell anything from food and clothing to electrical goods, plants and handicrafts. Traditional African wood carvings and copper and malachite jewellery from central Africa are sold on the pavements, along with local Zulu beadwork and basketry (41).

Away from the bustling sounds of the city, sun seekers are able to stroll along the Golden Mile, a six-kilometre promenade on the edge of the Indian Ocean. Anglers can throw their lines out from the piers and breakwaters, and catch fish for their families, while body boarders and surfers can enjoy the warm water and superb waves (38).

40

41

Colourful Zulu rickshas (40), the drivers adorned with beaded and feathered head-dresses, are among the more distinct features of the Golden Mile. The ricksha men with their lightly built two-wheel carts were once an integral part of the city's transport system when over a thousand plied the streets. Today a few survive only as a tourist drawcard.

Inland of Durban are the gentle KwaZulu-Natal Midlands, a fertile and temperate region midway between the coast and the gigantic Drakensberg mountain range. Cascading rivers cleave their way through the rolling green hills. One of the province's largest rivers, the Mgeni, crashes over the thunderous Howick Falls (42) on its way to the sea where it eventually flows out just north of Durban. Every year many people flock to see the spectacular Howick Falls and there are a number of picturesque picnic sites in the vicinity. This 93-metre-high waterfall is one of the most photographed falls in the country and is known to the African people as *kwaNogqaza*, which means 'place of the tall one'.

42

43

44

45

The mighty Drakensberg, or 'Dragon mountains', so named by the early Afrikaans settlers, pinnacles to a towering 3 000 metres above sea level on KwaZulu-Natal's western flank. Most of the range, including the awesome Amphitheatre (43), is protected as a national park. The Drakensberg is famed for its magnificent scenery, remarkable summer thunderstorms, winding

46

47

hiking paths, and flora and fauna. Apart from the sheer beauty of the mountains, other great attractions are the San paintings (44) of which more than 5 000 are to be found in the caves and crevices of the Drakensberg, and the rare bearded vulture (45) which can sometimes be seen soaring in the mountain thermals.

Zululand stretches north from the Tugela River and is renowned for its game reserves and wildlife, including the white rhinoceros (46) which has been saved from near extinction.

Some of the Nguni-speaking people made Zululand their home when they settled there and became famous under the great Zulu warrior-king, Shaka. Even today, in rural Zululand, the local people retain their traditions and consult their traditional healers (47), the *nyangas* and *sangomas*, in times of trouble.

The coastline is a perfect getaway for anglers, scuba divers and ski-boat enthusiasts. There are long beaches and incredible estuaries, such as the one at St Lucia (48) which flows in and out of the St Lucia lake system. This system is fed by both the sea and various rivers, and is home to a variety of fish.

48

49

50

Mpumalanga has its own distinct atmosphere and is laden with memories of pioneers, hunters and gold prospectors. The land boasts enormous mountains – an extension of the Drakensberg range, deep ravines, clear streams, waterfalls, wild flowers and wooded areas.

Alluvial gold drew thousands of diggers to the region in the late 1800s with the result that small towns flourished. However, the gold soon ran out, but, where the first significant gold strikes were made, the town of Pilgrim's Rest (49) was established. Once a gold town, then a forestry centre, the pretty town has now become a living museum.

The landscape is dotted with unusually shaped natural features, such as Bourke's Luck Potholes (50). Bourke, an early gold prospector, gave his name to the smoothly eroded limestone pools as he correctly surmised that the strange shapes were caused by the heavy alluvial gold dust which became trapped in them.

The Blyde River Canyon and its trio of sentinels, the Three Rondavels (51), are another of the

51

52

53

54

55

region's great natural wonders. The massive formations look out over the majestic red sandstone gorge and the winding river which has been dammed to create an expanse of lake that is now filled with hippos, crocodiles and a variety of other animals.

Part of the Kruger National Park, the most famous game reserve in Africa, falls within Mpumalanga while the remainder of the park is in the Northern Province. The natural splendours of this reserve have made it one of the world's greatest game and nature reserves and one of South Africa's major tourist destinations. It supports numerous bird, insect, reptile and mammal species, including the Big Five – the buffalo (52), the lion (54), the elephant (53), the rhinoceros and the leopard. The Big Five are so named because hunters consider them to be the five most dangerous wild animals which are sought after as trophies.

From small beginnings in 1927 when only a few people visited the reserve, the 1990s see the Kruger National Park as a sophisticated organisation which is able to cater for large numbers of visitors. Accommodation includes camping sites, chalets, huts and luxury cottages, and there are more than 3 000 kilometres of road to explore. Bateleur camp (55) is situated in the northern section of the park near a viewing platform which overlooks a permanent water hole. This affords excellent sightings of elephant wallowing in the muddy waters.

It is the presence of the Big Five, together with the thrill of seeing giraffe, hippo and huge herds of wildebeest and antelope in their magnificent natural surroundings, which continues to draw visitors from all over the world. The Kruger National Park is truly the jewel in the crown of southern African game reserves.

56

57

58

Johannesburg (56) is known to the African people as *eGoli*, or 'city of gold'. Founded on the discovery of gold just over a century ago, the city has become the financial and industrial centre of South Africa. Incorporating Soweto, the sprawling township lying to the south-west, Johannesburg is the largest city in southern Africa. It is a vibrant place and continues to grow. Today, more than 6 million people reside in this metropolis. Large, yellow slag heaps can be seen on the outskirts of the city; however these familiar square mountains are rapidly disappearing as new methods for extracting gold make it profitable to reprocess the old mine tailings.

59

The city is one of vast contrasts – from the affluent northern suburbs and the high-rise central business district and surrounding goldmines (58), to the dusty, overcrowded townships, many of whose residents struggle for basic facilities. Flashy shopping malls and waterfront complexes, such as the man-made Bruma Lake Mall (59) with its shops, restaurants and night spots, contrast sharply with the grubby open-air markets of downtown Johannesburg. Here vendors hustle a trade in anything from vegetables, shoes, pap (maize meal) and sauce, while traders in traditional *muthi* (medicine) (57) sell mixtures of indigenous plants, bark, roots, crocodile teeth and other animal parts.

Migrant workers coming to Johannesburg from the rural areas still follow their customs, consulting traditional healers and buying traditional medicines in the city's markets, despite the fact that they now live in one of South Africa's most sophisticated city centres.

60

61

62

63

While Johannesburg is known as the city of gold, Pretoria, a little over 50 kilometres to the north, is known as Jacaranda City. Every year the city bursts into bloom as the exquisite, lilac-flowered trees announce the arrival of spring and transform it into a cloud of soft, mauve blossoms (60). The attractive and sunny city is South Africa's administrative capital and is situated in a sheltered, warm region not far from the Magaliesberg Hills.

At the base of these lovely hills, is the popular Hartbeespoort Dam (61) to which city dwellers throng on warm days. This dam is a massive leisure area used by boating and fishing clubs as well as members of the general public. Wayside kiosks and farm stalls line the road to the dam and tearooms, camping grounds and other recreational facilities are available for weekend visitors.

Sun City is undeniably the entertainment mecca in the region. This hotel and resort complex offers just about everything a pleasure seeker could wish for. Set in the middle of the bleak bushveld, west of Johannesburg and Pretoria, this oasis of gardens, water features, luxurious hotels, glittering restaurants and vibrant night clubs throbs with activity. The Lost City, a fabulous addition to the complex, holds one of the country's finest golf courses as well as an enormous artificially created beach called the Valley of Waves (63), complete with sandy bathing area and rolling surf.

For culture of another kind, a visit to the rural areas in the north gives you a glimpse of an older Africa. This is home to many of the Ndebele people who are renowned for their colourful ceremonial dress, ornamentation and wall paintings (62). This lively spirit often spills over into the urban areas as soccer supporters dress in a style of eclectic fantasy (64).

64

65

66

In the eastern region of the Free State the landscape is dotted with attractive rolling farmlands, bright yellow sunflowers, fields of golden wheat, maize, cherries and peaches, interspersed with grasslands of grazing cattle and woolly sheep. Enormous weathered sandstone outcrops, tinted a range of autumn shades by the presence of iron oxides, rise up from the fields. A spectacular example of this is the Brandwag, or Sentinel (66), one of two 100-metre-high buttresses that form a gateway to the Golden Gate Highlands National Park.

The Basotho Cultural Village (65), situated close to the park, has been created to preserve the culture and traditional way of life of the Basotho, who live in both the Free State and the neighbouring (independent kingdom of) Lesotho. The park lies in the valley of the Little Caledon River and wild animals such as zebra, wildebeest, eland and oribi wander its lush grasslands and sandstone ridges. The beauty and fertility of the landscape, as typified by the country-side around the small village of Clarens (67), has drawn not only farmers but also artists and crafts people to the area.

67

68

69

In the Northern Cape the country becomes flatter and drier, but this did not deter the hundreds of diamond prospectors who rushed there when diamonds were discovered in and around the town of Kimberley in the 1870s. The discovery of diamonds on Colesberg Kopje started one of the greatest of all diamond rushes, and the result of the digging was the Big Hole in Kimberley (69).

Among the largest man-made holes in the world, the Big Hole has a surface area of 13,38 hectares, a depth of 1 079 metres and a perimeter of 1,6 kilometres. More than 28 million tons of earth were removed during the digging activities, yielding a total of 14 504 carats of diamonds before operations ceased on 14th August 1914. Over the years, water has slowly seeped in and partially fills the Big Hole.

Present-day Kimberley offers the visitor an atmosphere scented with old memories and dramas. Wandering around the marvellous Kimberley Mine Museum in which an entire street has been reconstructed, complete with a pub called the Digger's Rest (68), you can easily imagine days gone by when the area was bustling with flamboyant characters and dusty miners.

Further west, the dry country is broken by the great Orange River as it wends its way to the Atlantic Ocean. The river starts in the Lesotho Highlands and travels a distance of 2 250 kilometres across the high central plateau to spill out into the sea near the Namibian border on the west coast, close to Oranjemund. Around the lower reaches of the Orange River is the Augrabies Falls National Park, a wilderness area of 9 000 hectares. The centrepiece of this park is the awe-inspiring Augrabies Falls (70). At peak periods, when the river is in flood, water plunges through the nine-kilometre-long series of granite cataracts at a rate that is more than half that of Zimbabwe's Victoria Falls in flood.

70

71

72

The arid Kalahari is not a true desert, but a semi-desert savanna. In the dry season, animals tend to disperse in search of food which makes it a good time to see the nomadic herds of antelope, including the gemsbok with their long, elegant horns (71), eland, blue wildebeest and springbok.

The Kalahari Gemsbok National Park is the second largest national park in South Africa. It adjoins the Gemsbok National Park on the border with Botswana. There are no boundary fences and the animals have complete freedom of movement.

The pretty Twee Rivieren camp (72), one of the main camps in the park, is situated near the confluence of two major rivers, the Nossob and the Auob, and is an excellent place to see animals as well as an exciting variety of birds.

The landscape of the Cederberg, with its high peaks, rugged ridges and pristine natural vegetation, is rated by hikers and mountaineers as one of the most beautiful wilderness areas in South Africa. Although no large game species occur, it is possible to spot rhebok, klipspringer and baboon. Eerie rock shapes, such as the Wolfberg Arch (73), abundant flora and the clear atmosphere encourage nature lovers to explore this haunting countryside.

Beyond lie the arid plains of Namaqualand where every year, for a few weeks after the winter rains, the harsh terrain is transformed into a carpet of colour. A profusion of over 4 000 species of succulents, daisies and other plants burst into flower, enticing visitors to come and enjoy the riotously vivid fields of colour as seen at the Goegap Nature Reserve (74).

73

74

75

The coastal strip running from the Orange River down the west coast to Cape Town is, for a large part of the year, windswept and bleak, inhabited mainly by fishermen and vast colonies of Cape gannets and seals. The sand-blown shoreline is sparsely vegetated and the climate is influenced by the cold north-flowing Benguela Current in which marine life thrives.

Breeding colonies of gannets (76) have long been established on the small islands off the south-western coast, such as on Bird Island near Lamberts Bay. For centuries, phosphorous-rich guano deposits were scraped off the rocks to support the thriving fertiliser industry. This industry has largely closed down, leaving only the fishermen with their colourful rowing boats (75) to sustain the charming, and somewhat, melancholy coastal villages.

The West Coast is well known for its abundant seafood and restaurants which serve delicious delicacies like rock lobster (77), pulled fresh from the icy Atlantic waters.

76

77